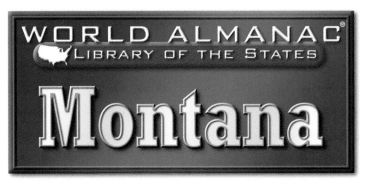

THE TREASURE STATE

by Kris Hirschmann

WORLD ALMANAC® LIBRARY

Please visit our web site at: www.worldalmanaclibrary.com
For a free color catalog describing World Almanac® Library's list of high-quality books and multimedia programs, call 1-800-848-2928 (USA) or 1-800-387-3178 (Canada). World Almanac® Library's fax: (414) 332-3567.

Library of Congress Cataloging-in-Publication Data

Hirschmann, Kris, 1967-
    Montana, the Treasure State / by Kris Hirschmann.
      p. cm. — (World Almanac Library of the states)
    Includes bibliographical references and index.
    Contents: Almanac — History — The people — The land — Economy & commerce — Politics & government — Culture & lifestyle — Notable people — Time line — State events & attractions — More about Montana.
    ISBN 0-8368-5153-6 (lib. bdg.)
    ISBN 0-8368-5324-5 (softcover)
    1. Montana—Juvenile literature. [1. Montana.] I. Title. II. Series.
F731.3.H57   2003
978.6—dc21
                                    2002038041

First published in 2003 by
World Almanac® Library
330 West Olive Street, Suite 100
Milwaukee, WI 53212 USA

Copyright © 2003 by World Almanac® Library.

A Creative Media Applications Production
Design: Alan Barnett, Inc.
Copy editor: Laurie Lieb
Fact checker: Joan Verniero
Photo researcher: Colin D. Scott
World Almanac® Library project editor: Tim Paulson
World Almanac® Library editors: Mary Dykstra, Gustav Gedatus, Jacqueline Laks Gorman, Lyman Lyons
World Almanac® Library art direction: Tammy Gruenewald
World Almanac® Library graphic designers: Scott M. Krall, Melissa Valuch

Photo credits: pp. 4-5 © CORBIS; p. 6 (left) © ArtToday; p. 6 (top right) © Dale C. Spartas/CORBIS; p. 6 (bottom right) © Buddy Mays/CORBIS; p. 7 (top) © ArtToday; p. 7 (bottom) © AP/Wide World Photos; p. 9 (both) © Bettmann/CORBIS; p. 10 © Hulton Archive/Getty Images; p. 11 © AP/Wide World Photos; p. 12 © Kevin R. Morris/CORBIS; p. 13 © Hulton Archive/Getty Images; p. 14 © AP/Wide World Photos; p. 15 © AP/Wide World Photos; p. 17 © Brian A. Vikander/CORBIS; p. 18 © AP/Wide World Photos; p. 19 © AP/Wide World Photos; p. 20 (left) © ArtToday; p. 20 (center) © Kevin R. Morris/CORBIS; p. 20 (right) © ArtToday; p. 21 (left) © ArtToday; p. 21 (center) © Michael S. Yamashita/CORBIS; p. 21 (right) © AP/Wide World Photos; p. 23 © CORBIS; p. 26 (left) © ArtToday; p. 26 (right) © Carol Cohen/CORBIS; p. 27 © Sheldan Collins/CORBIS; p. 29 © Michael S. Lewis/CORBIS; p. 31 (top) © CORBIS; p. 31 (bottom) © AP Photo/George Lane; p. 32 © AP/Wide World Photos; p. 33 © Dave G. Houser/CORBIS; p. 34 © Kevin R. Morris/CORBIS; p. 35 © AP/Wide World Photos; p. 36 © AP/Wide World Photos; p. 37 (top) © AP Photo/Bozeman Daily Chronicle, Deirdre Eitel; p. 37 (bottom) © AP/Wide World Photos; p. 38 © Bettmann/CORBIS; p. 39 (top) © Hulton Archive/Getty Images; p. 39 (top) © CORBIS; p. 39 (bottom) © CORBIS; p. 40 (bottom) © CORBIS; p. 41 (left) © Bettmann/CORBIS; p. 41 (right) © AP Photo/Stuart White; pp. 42-43 © Hulton Archive/Getty Images; p. 44 (top) © AP/Wide World Photos; p. 44 (bottom) © Brian A. Vikander/CORBIS; p. 45 (top) © Lindsay Hebberd/CORBIS; p. 45 (bottom) © AP/Wide World Photos

Printed in the United States of America

2 3 4 5 6 7 8 9 07 06 05 04 03

Montana

INTRODUCTION 4

ALMANAC 6

HISTORY 8

THE PEOPLE 16

THE LAND 20

ECONOMY & COMMERCE 24

POLITICS & GOVERNMENT 28

CULTURE & LIFESTYLE 32

NOTABLE PEOPLE 38

TIME LINE 42

STATE EVENTS & ATTRACTIONS 44

MORE ABOUT MONTANA 46

INDEX 47

Heart of the American Frontier

Since the early 1800s, when white settlers first began to flow into the region seeking furs, gold, and other natural riches, Montana has been a tapestry of cowboys, Native Americans, miners, bandits, and in general all things Western. Vast expanses of land in the east and towering mountains in the west were the perfect backdrop to the Montana frontier lifestyle, which emphasized inner toughness, independence, and an adventurous spirit.

The original rush to Montana occurred because of the state's abundant natural treasures, including wildlife, minerals (such as gold, silver, and copper), timber, and farm and ranch land. In early years, these natural riches were the basis of the state's economy as well as its history. Today natural resources continue to be important sources of jobs and income in Montana. However, since 1990, service industries (those in which services such as finance, retail sales, and tourism, rather than products, are sold) have overtaken goods as Montana's most important moneymaker.

As Montana's economy has shifted from resources to services, the state's gorgeous natural landscape has come into focus as perhaps its greatest natural treasure. With its towering mountains and lush forests, its desertlike badlands and waving wheat fields, Montana is an outdoors-lover's paradise. Combined with the state's relatively sparse population, Montana's landscape today attracts down-to-earth people who appreciate having open space and the freedom to be themselves.

In a very real way, Montana is the heart of the American frontier today, just as much as it was 150 years ago. The Montana lifestyle is not always easy. But for those who reside in "the last best state," as Montana has been called, it is the only life worth living.

▶ Map of Montana showing the interstate highway system, as well as major cities and waterways.

▼ In Montana's vast open expanses, the sky can appear huge. For this reason, the state is sometimes called "Big Sky Country."

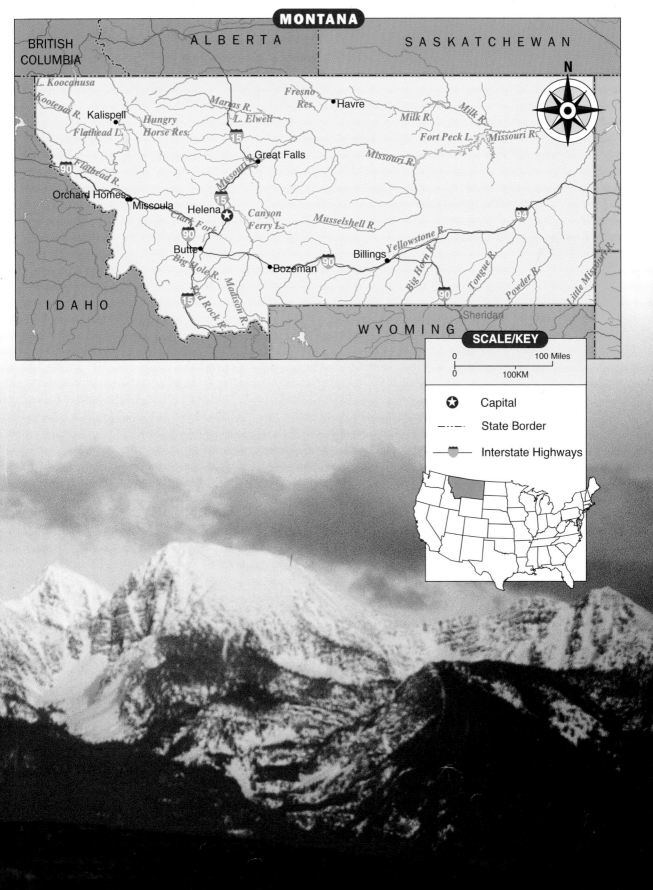

MONTANA

BRITISH COLUMBIA

ALBERTA

SASKATCHEWAN

N

L. Koocanusa

Kootenai R.

Kalispell

Flathead L.

Hungry Horse Res.

Marias R.

L. Elwell

Fresno Res.

Havre

Milk R.

Milk R.

Fort Peck L.

Missouri R.

15

Flathead R.

Great Falls

Missouri R.

Missouri R.

90

Orchard Homes

Missoula

Helena

15

Clark Fork

Canyon Ferry L.

Musselshell R.

94

Butte

90

Big Hole R.

Bozeman

90

Billings

Yellowstone R.

Big Horn R.

Tongue R.

Powder R.

Little Missouri R.

IDAHO

15

Red Rock R.

Madison R.

90

Sheridan

WYOMING

SCALE/KEY

0   100 Miles

0   100KM

★ Capital

State Border

Interstate Highways

Fast Facts

MONTANA (MT), The Treasure State

Entered Union
November 8, 1889 (41st state)

Capital	Population
Helena	25,780

Total Population (2000)
902,195 (44th most populous state)
— *Between 1990 and 2000, the state's population increased 12.9 percent.*

Largest Cities	Population
Billings	89,847
Missoula	57,053
Great Falls	56,690
Butte–Silver Bow	34,606
Bozeman	27,509

Land Area
145,552 square miles (376,980 square kilometers) (4th largest state)

State Motto
Oro y Plata — *Spanish for "Gold and Silver"*

State Song
"Montana" by Joseph E. Howard and Charles C. Cohan; adopted in 1945

State Bird
Western meadowlark — *Explorers Lewis and Clark sighted this bird on their first visit to Montana in 1805.*

State Fish
Blackspotted cutthroat trout

State Flower
Bitterroot — *The roots of this purplish-pink flower were important in the diet of Montana's Native Americans.*

State Grass
Bluebunch wheatgrass — *Found all over the state, bluebunch is important to Montana cattle and sheep ranchers as food for their animals.*

State Tree
Ponderosa pine — *Early settlers used the wood of this tree in most of their buildings.*

State Fossil
Maiasaur (duck-billed dinosaur) — *First found in Montana, fossilized remains of this animal proved that some dinosaurs laid eggs in nests and took care of their babies after they hatched.*

State Animal
Grizzly bear — *One of the nation's largest populations of grizzlies lives in Montana's Glacier National Park.*

State Gemstones
Sapphire and agate

C. M. Russell Museum, *Great Falls*

This museum complex contains the world's most complete collection of work by famed cowboy artist Charles Russell. Original paintings and sculptures are housed next door to the artist's historic log-cabin studio.

Glacier National Park, *northwest Montana*

This stunning national park features nearly fifty glaciers, more than two hundred lakes, broad glacier-carved valleys, and towering peaks. About 1.7 million tourists enjoy the park's scenery and outdoor activities each year.

Little Bighorn Battlefield National Monument, *Crow Agency*

Located on the Crow Reservation, this monument commemorates the Battle of the Little Bighorn. A visitor center displays artifacts and battle scene exhibits. Marble headstones mark the places where Custer's men fell during the fateful battle.

For other places and events, see p. 44.

BIGGEST, BEST, AND MOST

- Montana has more species of mammals (108) than any other U.S. state.

- Montana has the largest grizzly bear population in the lower forty-eight states.

- The most extreme temperature change ever recorded occurred in Browning, Montana, January 23–24, 1916. During a 24-hour period, the temperature dropped from 44°Fahrenheit (7°Celsius) to –56°F (–49°C).

STATE FIRSTS

- **1872** Yellowstone National Park in Wyoming, Idaho, and Montana was established as the nation's first national park.

- **1916** Montana's Jeannette Rankin became the first woman ever elected to the U.S. Congress.

Montana Is Dinosaur Country

One of the world's largest deposits of dinosaur fossils is located in Montana. The gigantic fossil bed is approximately 0.25 miles (0.4 kilometers) long and 1.25 miles (2 km) wide and contains the remains of up to ten thousand maiasaurs. Scientists believe that the maiasaurs died when a volcanic eruption blanketed the area in smoke, ash, and poisonous gases many millions of years ago.

Some of the most interesting fossils in the maiasaur bed are the preserved remains of maiasaur nests. Found by paleontologist Jack Horner in 1978, these fossilized nests support the theory that some dinosaurs protected their babies after they were born. Before Horner's discovery, scientists did not believe dinosaurs were intelligent enough for such behavior.

The Great Centennial Cattle Drive

Cattle are an important part of Montana's history and economy. When Montanans began planning their 1989 state centennial celebration, a commemorative cattle drive was included in the festivities. The Great Centennial Cattle Drive of 1989 began on September 4, 1989, when 3,600 horses and riders and more than 300 wagons drove 3,000 cattle down Main Street in the town of Roundup. It took six days to drive the herd 60 miles (97 km) from Roundup to Billings, where cheering crowds greeted the cattle's arrival.

Life on the Frontier

> I accept with pleasure . . . your congratulations on the acquisition of Louisiana. . . . The territory acquired . . . has more than doubled the area of the United States, and the new parts is [sic] not inferior to the old in soil, climate, productions and important communications.
>
> — *Thomas Jefferson in a letter to General Horatio Gates, upon the purchase of the land that includes most of present-day Montana, July 11, 1803*

Montana's first permanent residents were called the "late hunters." These people are believed to have arrived in present-day Montana about two thousand years ago. Ancient bison hunting sites, tepee circles, and cave drawings are a few of the remnants they left behind.

Modern-day Native peoples began migrating to the Montana area in the 1500s. The Kootenai, Salish (Flathead), and Pend d'Oreille people were the first to arrive. The Crow and the Shoshone arrived in the 1600s, and the Blackfoot, Assiniboin, and Gros Ventre appeared in the 1700s. The Yanktonai Sioux and the Northern Cheyenne moved into the area in the early 1800s. The Ojibwe (Chippewa) and Cree were the latest to arrive, appearing for the first time in the 1870s.

The European Years

In 1682, France became the first European country to claim ownership of the Montana area. Most of the state was included in France's Louisiana region, a huge swath of land that covered the midsection of the present-day continental United States.

The first European exploration of the Montana area was probably carried out in 1743 by French brothers François and Louis Joseph de la Vérendrye. The brothers found many natural riches, including beavers and other pelt animals. The Vérendryes' reports encouraged trappers and traders to enter the Montana area over the following years, but there were no organized expeditions.

Native Americans of Montana

- Assiniboin
- Blackfoot
- Cree
- Crow
- Gros Ventre
- Kalispel
- Kootenai
- Northern Cheyenne
- Ojibwe (Chippewa)
- Pend d'Oreille
- Salish (Flathead)
- Shoshone
- Yanktonai Sioux

DID YOU KNOW?

Early Montana-area peoples sometimes hunted mammoths. A large mammoth could weigh as much as 20,000 pounds (9,072 kilograms).

In 1803, French emperor Napoleon Bonaparte sold the Louisiana Territory to the United States for the sum of $15 million. The Louisiana Purchase, as the sale was called, included more than 800,000 square miles (2,072,000 km) of land west of the Mississippi River. The sale doubled the size of the United States and added the eastern portion of present-day Montana to U.S. territorial possessions.

Lewis and Clark

Following the Louisiana Purchase, President Thomas Jefferson organized an expedition to explore the new U.S. territory. The Expedition, called the Corps of Discovery, was headed by Meriwether Lewis and William Clark. It including about forty soldiers, guides, and interpreters. The Expedition departed St. Louis, Missouri, on May 14, 1804.

Lewis and Clark's men traveled up the Missouri River and reached the border of present-day Montana in April 1805. They passed through the heart of Montana and eventually reached the river's headwaters in the Rocky Mountains. Continuing westward from the Rockies, they traveled all the way to the Pacific Ocean, then turned around and headed toward home.

▼ Meriwether Lewis (lower left) and William Clark (lower right) headed the Corps of Discovery, the first official U.S. expedition to explore the Louisiana Territory.

Now moving eastward, Lewis and Clark's Expedition passed through Montana again in 1806. This time the Expedition split into two groups. Lewis's group followed the Marias River in the north, while Clark's group followed the Yellowstone River in the south. The groups reunited on the Missouri River near the North Dakota border and arrived home in St. Louis on September 23, 1806.

Trappers and Traders

Lewis and Clark kept good notes throughout their travels. Their notes included accounts of the many beavers, otters, and other pelt animals in the Montana region.

The first person to act on Lewis and Clark's information was a Spaniard named Manuel Lisa. Rushing westward, he set up Fort Manuel Lisa — Montana's first trading post — at the mouth of the Bighorn River. Other trappers and traders followed Lisa's lead, and trading posts soon dotted the Montana landscape. Two of the most important posts were Fort Union, built in 1829, and Fort Benton, built in 1847.

While the fur frenzy continued, the U.S. government was negotiating with Britain over land ownership in what is now the northwest continental United States. In the Oregon Treaty of 1846, the two nations agreed that the northwest portion of present-day Montana, among other regions, would become U.S. territory. With this agreement, all of current-day Montana was now in the possession of the United States.

The Montana Gold Rush

Around the same time, rumors arose that there was gold in what is now southwest Montana. A stream of prospectors began trickling into the area from the East to try their luck.

Montana's gold rush started in earnest in 1862, when rich deposits of gold were found on Grasshopper Creek near the Beaverhead River. Within months, the town of Bannack rose to support the hordes of prospectors flooding to the area. Another major find was made in 1863 at Alder Gulch, just 75 miles

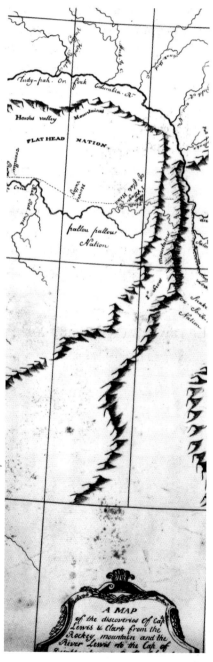

▶ This map created by the Corps of Discovery during the Lewis and Clark Expedition shows a portion of the Missouri River.

(121 km) east of Bannack. Alder Gulch yielded $10 million in gold in its first year.

Other gold strikes soon followed the Grasshopper Creek and Alder Gulch discoveries. Last Chance Gulch, Confederate Gulch, Grizzly Gulch, and Rattlesnake Gulch were just a few of the prospecting communities that arose across the territory.

Montana Territory

Gold was not the only draw in Montana. Settlers also came to hunt buffalo, graze cattle, and farm the land. With no rules to speak of, life in the Montana region was rough and competitive. Emotions ran high as thousands fought for their share of Montana's natural riches.

With its growing and unruly population of non-Native settlers, Montana clearly needed government. In 1863, Congress established the Idaho Territory, which included present-day Idaho and Montana. However, the territory proved too large to be governed effectively. Recognizing this problem, Congress broke off the area that is now Montana and declared it the Montana Territory on May 26, 1864.

In December 1864, Montana's first territorial assembly was held in Bannack. Hoping to tame the rowdy population, delegates met for sixty days and passed several hundred pages of laws.

The Battle of the Little Bighorn

As Montana became more and more settled, trouble began to brew between the settlers and the area's Native tribes. The growing non-Native population, which made liberal use of the Natives' traditional resources, was one problem. An even bigger problem, however, was the repeated breaking of treaties between the United States and the Natives by settlers throughout the West.

The seeds of major trouble were planted in Dakota Territory in the early 1870s. Gold had been discovered in the Black Hills, and

Sacagawea

Lewis and Clark's Expedition included a Shoshone woman named Sacagawea. She was the wife of Toussaint Charbonneau, a French Canadian who was hired by Lewis and Clark as an interpreter. With her infant boy strapped to her back, Sacagawea accompanied her husband and the Corps of Discovery across Montana, sharing all the hardships of the journey.

Sacagawea's presence proved invaluable when Lewis and Clark reached the Rocky Mountains. There she gained the help of her Shoshone kin in guiding the group through the mountainous region. Without the Shoshones' help, it is unlikely that Lewis and Clark's Expedition could have found its way.

Today Sacagawea's contributions are honored by monuments at Three Forks and Armstead, Montana. Her image also appears on the U.S. one-dollar coin.

non-Native settlers rushed to the area in the hopes of getting rich. According to the 1868 Fort Laramie Treaty, however, the Black Hills belonged to the Sioux people. The U.S. government dealt with this obstacle by ordering the Sioux out of the Black Hills and onto reservations, in direct violation of the 1868 treaty. All Native people were ordered to reach the reservations no later than January 31, 1876.

In June 1876, the government learned that a group of Sioux and Cheyenne were living along Montana's Little Bighorn River. On June 25, Lieutenant Colonel George Armstrong Custer marched about two hundred soldiers into the area with the assignment of forcing the Native group onto reservations. Custer was not aware, however, that his soldiers were badly outnumbered. In the battle that followed, Custer and all of his men were killed.

Although the Battle of the Little Bighorn was considered a victory by Native peoples throughout the West, it was a great loss in the long run. The U.S. War Department sent huge numbers of military personnel west to enforce its

Missionaries in Montana

Catholicism first came to Montana at the request of the Salish Indians. Tribe members had heard about the church's mysterious "black robes" (priests) from Catholic traders, and they wanted one of their own. Their wish was granted in 1841 when Father Pierre Jean de Smet traveled from Missouri to establish St. Mary's Mission in the Bitterroot Valley. A few years later, de Smet helped to establish the St. Ignatius Mission near Flathead Lake.

Below: St. Mary's Mission, built in 1841 by Pierre Jean de Smet, is the site of Montana's first church and the state's first pharmacy. In 1866 the mission buildings were restored by Father Ravalli.

policies toward the Natives. Within a few years, all of the remaining Plains tribes had been forced onto reservations. There they were required to live in a way that did not interfere with the settlers' exploitation of the land.

The War of the Copper Kings

Meanwhile, a war of another sort was erupting in southwestern Montana. The seeds of the conflict were planted in the early 1870s when copper was discovered near the town of Butte. In 1881, Marcus Daly opened a copper mine in Butte and a smelter in nearby Anaconda to process the valuable material. Daly quickly became wealthy, and Butte Hill yielded so much copper that it became known as "the richest hill on Earth."

Others soon joined the copper-mining fray. Most notable were banker William Clark and engineer F. Augustus Heinze. Like Daly, these men soon became rich and powerful. Before long, the trio of Daly, Clark, and Heinze virtually ruled the state of Montana. Together, these men were known as the Copper Kings. Over the next few decades, the Copper Kings' rivalry became the stuff of legends as the three men fought for wealth and influence.

Marcus Daly was the ultimate winner of the struggle. Daly's Anaconda Copper Company absorbed the companies of the other two men and became so powerful that it was known simply as "The Company."

Growth and Statehood

Mining interests in Montana did more than just create wealth. They also brought railroads, notably the Northern Pacific Railway, to the state. The trains were needed to ship minerals out of the state. They also gave rise to farming and ranching communities and created a demand for coal, which was also mined in Montana. The territory's population continued to rise as industry built on industry to create opportunity for settlers.

As Montana's population and industries grew, so did talk of statehood. In 1884, Montanans appealed to Congress for statehood status. On November 8, 1889, Montana's proposed constitution was approved by Congress, and Montana became the nation's forty-first state.

Chief Joseph and the Nez Percé

One of the final major conflicts between the United States and Native Americans took place in Montana. The incident started early in 1877, when U.S. troops were instructed to move eight hundred Nez Percé from their Oregon home to a reservation in Idaho. Led by Chief Joseph, the Nez Percé escaped from the U.S. forces and fled. The soldiers caught up with the Nez Percé in Big Hole Valley, Montana. A fight broke out. Many Nez Percé were killed, but many escaped.

On October 5, 1877, U.S. forces caught up with the Nez Percé again near the present-day town of Chinook. After several days of battle, Chief Joseph surrendered to the U.S. troops with these words: "Hear me, my chiefs. I am tired. My heart is sick and sad. From where the sun now stands, I will fight no more forever."

Boom and Bust

Montana's growth picked up pace in the early 1900s, when advertising campaigns promising free land drew thousands of farmers to the new state. In just ten years, the state's population increased by about 60 percent.

Farming, however, can be an undependable business. Despite the fact that U.S. participation in World War I (1914–1918) greatly increased demand for Montana's products, many of Montana's new farmers discovered that they could not make a living on the 320 acres (130 hectares) of land allotted to each adult. To make matters worse, a severe drought in 1918 wiped out most crops. Unable to make a living, many farmers headed back East.

Just eleven years later, in 1929, the Great Depression struck throughout the United States. Demand for Montana's raw materials dropped, and industries throughout the state suffered. By 1935, one-fourth of all Montana residents were collecting federal relief money.

Substantial recovery occurred during the years of World War II (1939–1945), when demand once again rose for Montana's products. Old industries picked up, and new jobs were created, mostly in cities such as Billings, Missoula, and Great Falls. For the first time, Montana's urban population grew to outnumber its rural population.

The Postwar Era

After World War II, the focus of Montana industry shifted. Coal, oil, and gas became more important than gold, silver, copper, and timber, the state's traditional economic mainstays. New mining techniques helped companies extract valuable metals from the ground faster than ever before. Oil drilling sites peppered Montana's eastern region.

The new mining techniques created great wealth, but they also created environmental damage. In the early 1970s, Montana passed laws to reduce this damage. One law forced mining companies to replant the ground after they had removed minerals. Another raised taxes on mineral extraction. Laws like these marked the start of a strong environmental movement that exists in Montana to this day.

▲ The Northern Lights dance in the sky over Billings, Montana's largest city.

Birth of the Cattle Industry

Cattleman Nelson Story is credited with founding Montana's range-cattle industry. After finding gold in Virginia City in 1866, Story headed to Texas, where he used his new wealth to purchase three thousand longhorn cattle. He then hired thirty cowboys to help him drive his herd north.

To reach Montana, Story and his men had to travel through the heart of Indian country. Fearing for the group's safety, the U.S. Army tried to stop the drive. However, Story was determined. He avoided the army by traveling at night. After enduring encounters with Indians and other hardships, Story, his men, and the cattle eventually made it to Montana. The animals were turned loose on grazing pastures, and a new industry was born.

Despite the new restrictions, mining companies did well during the 1970s, when a worldwide energy shortage raised the demand for oil products. Once again, Montana's population boomed. The boom, however, was short-lived. The 1980s brought a drop in oil prices and a decrease in demand for copper. Faced with plummeting profits, the once mighty Anaconda Copper Mining Company closed its doors for good in 1983. The job shortage resulting from this and other closings forced many residents to leave the state, and Montana's population dropped from 826,000 in 1985 to 799,065 in 1990.

Montana Today

The 1990s were another recovery period for Montana. During this decade, the state's service industries (including tourism, finance, government, and other businesses that deal in services rather than goods) grew greatly, creating new jobs and attracting many new residents.

Montana today is a growing, vibrant state where both urban and rural communities have important places in the state's economy and culture. State politicians, developers, and residents look to the future but do not forget Montana's western roots, which are an important part of the state's history and personality.

Henry Plummer

In 1863, Henry Plummer was elected sheriff of the gold-mining town of Bannack. At the same time, Plummer secretly organized a group of bandits that became known as the Road Agents. The Road Agents tracked every shipment of gold out of Bannack and stole as much as they could, sometimes violently. Within a few months of Plummer's election, the gang had robbed and killed at least 102 men traveling the main route between Bannack and Virginia City. The Road Agents' reign of terror lasted until January 10, 1864, when Plummer was seized by angry citizens and hanged.

▼ Modern mining methods have stripped the earth of vegetation at this copper mine near Billings.

Elbowroom

> Where is there more opportunity than in Montana . . . to enjoy the elemental values of living, bright sun and clean air and space? We have room. We can be neighbors without getting in each other's hair. We can be individuals.
>
> — *Joseph Kinsey Howard*, Montana: High, Wide, and Handsome, *1959*

With 902,195 residents spread across 145,552 square miles (376,980 sq km) of land, Montana is one of the most sparsely populated U.S. states. Montana has an average population density of just 6.2 people per square mile (2.4 per square km), compared to 79.6 per square mile (30.7 per square km) for the United States as a whole. The population is split almost evenly between urban and rural residents.

Nearly all of Montana's major cities are located in the state's mountainous west. Billings, the state's largest city, sits at the edge of the Rockies about halfway across the state. Other major cities include Missoula, Great Falls, Butte, Bozeman, and Helena, all of which are in the west. In the year 2000, about 333,000 people (approximately

Age Distribution in Montana
(2000 Census)

Age	Population
0–4	54,869
5–19	202,571
20–24	58,379
25–44	245,220
45–64	220,207
65 & over	120,949

Across One Hundred Years

Montana's three largest foreign-born groups for 1890 and 1990

| ■ 1890 | ■ 1990 |

| Canada/Newfoundland 9,040 | Ireland 6,648 | England 6,480 |

Total state population: 132,159
Total foreign-born: 43,096 (32.6%)

| Canada 3,929 | Germany 1,381 | United Kingdom 1,137 |

Total state population: 799,065
Total foreign-born: 13,779 (1.7%)

Patterns of Immigration

The total number of people who immigrated to Montana in 1998 was 299. Of that number, the largest immigrant groups were from China (14%), Canada (13.4%), and Mexico (7%).

37 percent of Montana's population) lived in the state's ten largest cities.

Montana's geography forces a division of jobs and lifestyles. The flat lands of the east support farmers, ranchers, and other rural workers. Miners, service industry professionals, and other nonagricultural workers are found mostly in and around the mountains of the west.

Most Montanans trace their ancestry to Europe. Germany, Ireland, England, and the Scandinavian countries are especially well represented. Asians, African Americans, and other minorities are extremely rare in Montana, which has one of the least ethnically diverse populations of any U.S. state. Native Americans are by far Montana's largest minority, making up 6.2 percent of the state's population.

▲ Ranch hands relax at a campsite during a cattle drive in the Big Belt Mountains.

The Native Population

In 2000, Montana's Native population included 56,068 individuals. About two-thirds of the state's Native residents live on one of Montana's seven reservations. The remaining one-third are scattered throughout the rest of the state. Although one intended objective of the reservations is to preserve Native ways of life by keeping communities and traditions alive, the reality of reservation life can be quite different. The reservations have long represented various

DID YOU KNOW?

Many celebrities have Montana homes. TV mogul Ted Turner, actress Meg Ryan, and actress/model Andie MacDowell are just a few of the stars who live part-time in this state.

Heritage and Background, Montana   Year 2000

▶ Here is a look at the racial backgrounds of Montanans today. Montana ranks last among U.S. states with regard to African Americans as a percentage of the population.

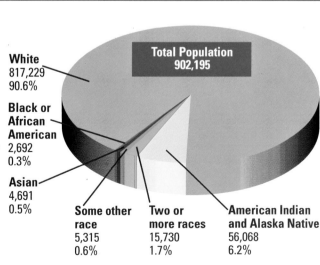

Total Population 902,195

White 817,229 90.6%

Black or African American 2,692 0.3%

Asian 4,691 0.5%

Native Hawaiian and Other Pacific Islander 470 0.1%

Some other race 5,315 0.6%

Two or more races 15,730 1.7%

American Indian and Alaska Native 56,068 6.2%

Note: 2.0% (18,081) of the population identify themselves as **Hispanic** or **Latino,** a cultural designation that crosses racial lines. Hispanics and Latinos are counted in this category as well as the racial category of their choice.

government policies of confinement and neglect, creating conditions that can promote poverty and alcoholism. To bring much-needed income into their societies, most reservations have established Native-run casinos that attract both locals and visitors. Many reservations also make money by exploiting their own land through mining, lumbering, and other resource-based industries.

Religion

About half of the residents of Montana are connected with organized religious groups. Protestantism is the dominant religion. Its adherents are scattered among several

Educational Levels of Montana Workers (age 25 and over)	
Less than 9th grade	25,200
9th to 12th grade, no diploma	50,158
High school graduate, including equivalency	183,415
Some college, no degree or associate degree	184,887
Bachelor's degree	100,758
Graduate or professional degree	42,203

▼ Traditional Native dress and dances are on display at the annual North American Indian Days Celebration. Tribes from the United States and Canada attend the competition sponsored by the Blackfoot Nation of Browning.

denominations, including Lutheranism and Methodism. The largest single religious denomination is Roman Catholicism, which has more adherents than any single Protestant denomination. The Mormon faith has a growing presence in the state.

Montana is also home to a unique religious group called the Hutterites, who are similar to the Amish of Pennsylvania. They follow a quiet, rural way of life outside the mainstream of society, practicing their own religion. The German-speaking Hutterites have established approximately forty colonies in Montana, each with sixty to one hundred members.

▲ Hutterites follow a strict dress code as part of their religious practices. They maintain a life of hard work on farms.

Education

Public education came to Montana in 1865, when the state's first territorial legislative assembly passed an act that created a school system. The first public school was opened later that same year in Virginia City.

Today, nearly nine hundred public elementary and secondary schools in Montana enroll more than 157,000 students. Montana's students consistently rank among the highest in the nation on standardized tests of reading, writing, math, and science achievement. Montana also has the eighth-highest high school completion rate in the United States.

In addition to its elementary and secondary schools, Montana has an excellent state university system that includes the University of Montana at Missoula, Montana State University in Bozeman, and four other campuses across the state. Private colleges include Carroll College in Helena and Rocky Mountain College in Billings.

Going to Extremes

In recent years, Montana has earned a reputation as a haven for extremist groups. Groups such as the Militia of Montana and the Montana Freemen are antigovernment organizations that support citizens' rights to bear arms and train in unofficial military maneuvers. These and other extremist groups may also work through government channels to reduce gay and ethnic rights, ban certain reading materials, and weaken or eliminate gun-control laws.

A State Divided

> It seems to me that Montana is a great splash of grandeur. The scale is huge but not overpowering. The land is rich with grass and color, and the mountains are the kind I would create if mountains were ever put on my agenda.
>
> — *John Steinbeck,* Travels with Charley: In Search of America, *1962*

With a total land area of 145,552 square miles (376,980 sq km), Montana is the fourth-largest U.S. state. Only Alaska, Texas, and California are larger. Montana is bordered by Idaho to the west and southwest, Wyoming to the south, North Dakota and South Dakota to the east, and Canada to the north. The state is mostly rectangular but shares a jagged border with Idaho.

Geographically, Montana is a state divided. The western third of the state is mountainous, part of the Rocky Mountains region. The eastern two-thirds of the state is mostly flat, part of the Great Plains region. Elevations range from a high of 12,799 feet (3,901 meters) atop Granite Peak in the southwest to a low of 1,800 feet (549 m) on the Kootenai River near the state's northwestern border.

The West

The Rocky Mountains run down the western side of Montana. Montana's Rockies have more than fifty distinct ranges. The mountaintops in many of these ranges are

Highest Point
Granite Peak
12,799 feet (3,901 m) above sea level

DID YOU KNOW?

Montana's name comes from the Spanish word *montaña,* which means "mountain." Yet mountains account for only about one-third of Montana's land area.

▼ *From left to right*: Montana mountains; Bighorn sheep; grizzly bear; moose; wheat fields; American bison (buffalo).

covered with snow eight to ten months a year, and a few active glaciers can be found at higher altitudes.

The mountain peaks in northwest Montana are packed together more tightly than those in the southwest. In the northwest, narrow valleys between 1 and 5 miles wide (1.6 and 8 km wide) separate the peaks. In the southwest, the valleys are wider, ranging from 30 to 40 miles (48 to 64 km) in width.

In terms of climate, western Montana is an extension of the Pacific Northwest. The towering Rockies trap moisture from the Pacific Ocean, creating a damp, temperate climate. This type of climate is excellent for trees and plant life, which abound in Montana's Rocky Mountain region.

The Rocky Mountain region of Montana is preserved for visitors in Glacier National Park. The park is located on the Canadian border in the northwestern portion of the state. Over 1 million acres (404,700 ha) of Montana's rugged mountains lie within the park's borders. The park gets its name from about fifty glaciers that dot its valleys. These massive sheets of ice are responsible for carving the valleys and peaks of Montana's western mountains. The smallest glaciers in the park occupy only a few acres. The largest ice masses cover several square miles. In addition, the park contains over 250 lakes that are fed by glacial activity. Glacier National Park has been designated an International Biosphere Reserve in an effort to protect the ecosystems found in this portion of the Rocky Mountains.

The East

Where the Rockies end, the Plains begin. The eastern two-thirds of Montana lies squarely within the Great Plains region, a grassy plateau that runs from the country's northern border all the way down through Texas. In Montana, the Plains region features gently rolling hills and

Average January temperature
Baker: 14°F (-10°C)
Kalispell: 21°F (-6°C)

Average July temperature
Baker: 73°F (23°C)
Kalispell: 64°F (18°C)

Average yearly rainfall
Baker:
  13.9 inches (35.3 cm)
Kalispell:
  16.5 inches (41.9 cm)

Average yearly snowfall
Baker:
  20 inches (50.8 cm)
Kalispell:
  65 inches (165.1 cm)

DID YOU KNOW?

Fort Peck Dam on the Missouri River is one of the world's biggest earth-fill dams. When the dam was built in 1940, it backed up the waters of the Missouri and created Fort Peck Lake.

Largest Lakes

Fort Peck Lake
240,000 acres
  (97,200 hectares)

Flathead Lake
125,000 acres
  (50,625 ha)

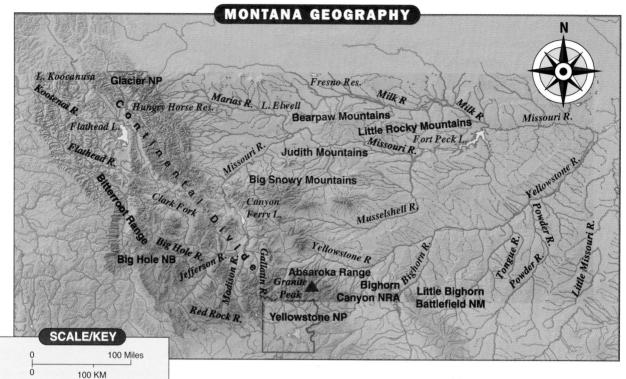

SCALE/KEY

```
0          100 Miles
0        100 KM
```

NP	National Park
NB	National Battlefield
NRA	National Recreation Area
NM	National Monument
▲	Highest Point
▲	Important Peaks
▦	Mountains

broad river valleys. The flat lands of the east seem to go on forever, and the eye is drawn upward to the expanse of sky overhead. This optical trick is the reason for one of Montana's best-known nicknames: "Big Sky Country."

The rolling Plains of the east are broken up in a few places by small groups of mountains. Eastern mountains include the Bear Paws, Big Snowy, Judith, and the Little Rocky Mountains. The southeast also contains Montana's badlands, where wind and water scour the landscape to create natural stone columns.

The climate in the east is much dryer than in the west. Temperatures are also more extreme, rising higher in the summer and dropping lower in the winter. Lacking the consistent rains of the west, plant life is much sparser in the east than in the Rocky Mountain region. Wild grasses that require little water, however, grow well; so do wheat and other important crops.

Major Rivers

Missouri River
2,315 miles (3,726 km)

Yellowstone River
682 miles (1,098 km)

Clark Fork River
300 miles (483 km)

Rivers and Lakes

One of Montana's most important geological features is the Continental Divide. This imaginary line runs along the crests of various mountains in the Rockies region. Rivers to the east of the Divide empty eventually into the Atlantic Ocean and its related seas, while rivers to the west empty into the Pacific.

Montana's two largest rivers flow toward the east. One of these rivers is the Missouri, a major tributary of the Mississippi. The Missouri originates where the Jefferson, Gallatin, and Madison Rivers come together at Three Forks in southwestern Montana. The state's second largest river is the Yellowstone, a tributary that feeds into the Missouri just past the North Dakota border. A third major river, the Clark Fork, flows toward the west.

Although no major rivers are involved, a small area in the north-central part of Montana drains into the Arctic Ocean via Hudson Bay in Canada. Montana is the only U.S. state that drains into three oceans.

Montana also includes two major lakes. Fort Peck Lake, an artificially created reservoir in the northeast, is the state's largest lake. Flathead Lake in the northwest, a natural body of water, is the state's other large lake.

Wildlife

The Rocky Mountain region teems with animal life — grizzly bears, Rocky Mountain goats, bighorn sheep, moose, mountain lions, elk, deer, black bears, beavers, and a variety of small mammals. The eastern part of the state is home to deer, coyotes, prairie dogs, and other small mammals.

In addition to its many interesting mammals, nearly four hundred species of birds make their home in Montana. More than eighty species of game fish make the rivers of Montana a fishing paradise.

Great Quake

In 1959, an earthquake measuring 7.3 on the Richter scale shook Montana. About 80 million tons (about 73 million metric tons) of rock slid into the Madison River near Virginia City. Today the quake is memorialized by the Madison Canyon Earthquake Area, where visitors can view the natural dam and lake created by the landslide.

▼ Mountain lions, also known as cougars, are solitary animals that find Montana's back country an ideal environment no matter what the season.

From Fur to Tourism

> We have this great commercial advantage in having the most fertile soil and the richest mines yet known to man.
>
> — *W. B. George, Chairman of the Executive Committee of the Good Roads Convention, speaking at the convention's opening, June 16, 1910*

Montana's economy has changed greatly since the 1800s. In its earliest days, the economy was based largely on the fur trade. Mining for gold, silver, and copper became important in the 1860s. The growing miner population encouraged the growth of ranches and eventually farms, whose products were needed to support the extra people.

Mining and agriculture were the mainstays of Montana's economy until the mid-1900s, when service industries began growing in importance. The growth of tourism over the past few decades has also contributed greatly to Montana's economy.

Services

Today, Montana's economy is mostly service-based. Important services include finance, insurance, and real estate; wholesale and retail trade; and transportation, communications, and utilities. Together, these services accounted for 42.1 percent of Montana's gross state product (the total value of goods and services produced) in 2000.

Tourism is also an important service industry in Montana, earning $1.6 billion per year. Tourism operations are located mostly in the western part of the state, where people come to enjoy Glacier National Park, Yellowstone Park, and other natural wonders. Snow skiing at resorts such as Big Mountain and Big Sky is also becoming increasingly popular among tourists looking to avoid the Colorado crowds.

Government rounds out Montana's service industries.

Top Employers
(of workers age sixteen and over)

Services	43.9%
Wholesale and retail trade	15.8%
Agriculture, forestry, fisheries, and mining	7.9%
Manufacturing	6.0%
Transportation, communications, and other public utilities	7.6%
Construction	7.4%
Federal, state, and local government (including military)	5.9%
Finance, insurance, and real estate	5.5%

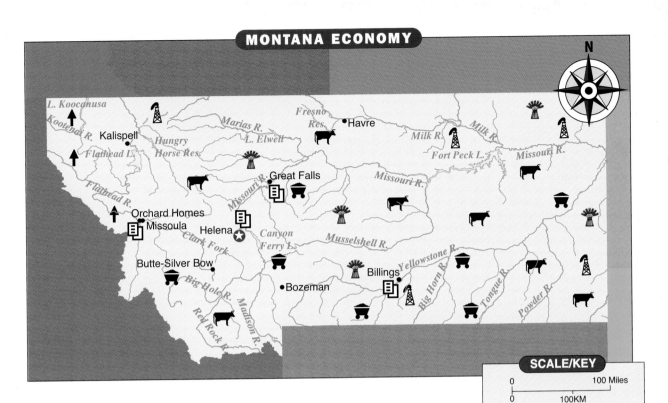

SCALE/KEY

0   100 Miles
0   100KM

- Cattle/Dairy
- Farming
- Forestry
- Mining
- Oil/Natural Gas
- Services

Montana Gross State Product   Millions of dollars

Total gross state product
$21,777

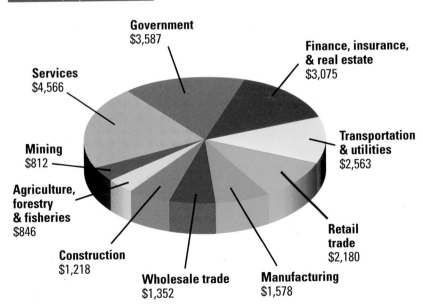

Government
$3,587

Finance, insurance,
& real estate
$3,075

Services
$4,566

Transportation
& utilities
$2,563

Mining
$812

Agriculture,
forestry
& fisheries
$846

Retail
trade
$2,180

Construction
$1,218

Wholesale trade
$1,352

Manufacturing
$1,578

Montana's federal, state, local, and military government operations accounted for 16.5 percent of the gross state product in 2000.

Manufacturing

Manufacturing is the next most important sector of Montana's economy. Manufacturing operations contributed 7.2 percent of the gross state product in 2000.

Most manufacturing in Montana involves the processing of the state's natural resources, particularly timber, minerals, and raw foods. Timber from the western forests is transformed into lumber, furniture, and paper products, which are then sold out of state. (Montana lumber also contributes to a booming construction industry, which itself contributed 5.6 percent of the gross state product in 2000.) Petroleum and coal likewise are processed for outside sale. Cattle are processed into beef products for the national market. Cow's milk is processed into diary products. Wheat and other crops are also packaged for shipment and sale.

Agriculture

Agriculture, forestry, and fisheries accounted for a combined 3.9 percent of Montana's gross state product in 2000. Most of the income in this category comes from agriculture, and the agricultural income is evenly split between livestock and crops. Cattle provide the largest part of the livestock income. In 2000, there were 2.6 million cattle in Montana, or about three per human resident. Dairy products, pigs, and sheep also make important contributions to Montana's livestock income. In terms of crop income, wheat is the major contributor. (In 2000, Montana ranked third among the wheat-producing states in the country.) Other important crop products include barley, hay, and sugar beets.

Made in Montana

Leading farm products and crops
Cattle and calves
Wheat
Barley
Hay
Sugar beets

Other products
Lumber and wood products
Petroleum products
Processed foods

▼ *Left*: Hikers enjoy an outing on one of Montana's many hiking trails. *Right*: The ghost town of Bannack is a popular tourist attraction.

▲ Six mining companies paid seventy-eight million dollars to the federal government for the cleanup of the Berkley Pit Mine near Butte-Silverbow.

Although agriculture contributes only a modest portion of Montana's gross state product, it takes up a huge amount of the available land. About two-thirds of the state's land is devoted to farming and ranching.

Natural Resources

Mining, once the heart and soul of Montana commerce, today plays a lesser role in the state's economy. Although it is still important, mining now ranks last among the state's major industries, bringing in about 3.7 percent of the state's income in 2000.

Oil and gas account for the largest part of Montana's mining income. Next in importance are coal and then metals, including copper, gold, lead, silver, and zinc. Nonmetallic minerals, including gemstones such as sapphires, garnets, and agates, contribute a smaller portion of the state's mining income.

Besides mining, timber is Montana's most important natural resource. Forests cover about 23 million acres (9.3 million ha) of Montana's land area. Of this total, about 14 million acres (5.7 million ha) support commercial logging operations.

Montana Mining Restrictions

In the early days of mining, companies tunneled underground to extract minerals. In the 1950s, however, underground tunnels were replaced by a technique called strip mining. In this method, soil is sifted to expose mineral deposits, then returned to the ground once the minerals have been harvested.

In the early 1970s, Montanans pushed for stricter regulations on strip mining operations. Laws such as the Montana Environmental Policy Act, the Major Facility Siting Act, and the Strip Mine Reclamation Act were passed to protect the land. Among other things, these acts require mine owners to pay a higher tax and to clean up a site after extracting minerals. Environmental legislation protects the land that Montanans feel is essential to their quality of life.

Major Airports		
Airport	**Location**	**Passengers per year (2001)**
Billings Logan International	Billings	707,871
Gallatin Field	Bozeman	512,396
Missoula International	Missoula	485,094

Power to the Citizens

> Be it ordained . . . that on behalf of the people of Montana, we in convention assembled, do adopt the constitution of the United States.
>
> — *Montana Ordinance No. 1, February 22, 1889*

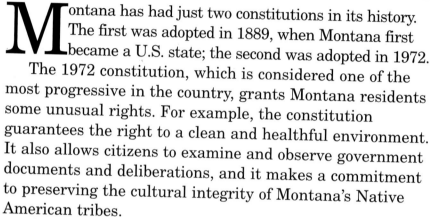

Montana has had just two constitutions in its history. The first was adopted in 1889, when Montana first became a U.S. state; the second was adopted in 1972.

The 1972 constitution, which is considered one of the most progressive in the country, grants Montana residents some unusual rights. For example, the constitution guarantees the right to a clean and healthful environment. It also allows citizens to examine and observe government documents and deliberations, and it makes a commitment to preserving the cultural integrity of Montana's Native American tribes.

Perhaps most important, Montana's citizens have the right to make or reject amendments to the state constitution. To do either, a petition must be signed by at least 5 percent of the voters in at least one-third of Montana's voting districts, and the total number of signers must equal at least 5 percent of the voters in the state. When these requirements are met, the petition is filed and then voted on by all of the state's citizens.

The system of government in Montana — just like that of the U.S. federal government — is divided into three branches: executive, legislative, and judicial. The executive branch administers laws, the legislative branch makes laws, and the judicial branch interprets and enforces laws. In addition to the state government, Montana's Native American tribes have their own federally recognized governments.

The Executive Branch

The executive branch includes the governor, lieutenant governor, secretary of state, attorney general, superintendent

State Constitution

"**W**e the people of Montana grateful to God for the quiet beauty of our state, the grandeur of our mountains, the vastness of our rolling plains, and desiring to improve the quality of life, equality of opportunity and to secure the blessings of liberty for this and future generations do ordain and establish this constitution."

— *Preamble to the 1972 Montana State Constitution*

Elected Posts in the Executive Branch		
Office	Length of Term	Term Limits
Governor	4 years	8 years in any 16-year period
Lieutenant Governor	4 years	8 years in any 16-year period
Secretary of State	4 years	8 years in any 16-year period
Attorney General	4 years	8 years in any 16-year period
Superintendent of Public Instruction	4 years	8 years in any 16-year period
Auditor	4 years	8 years in any 16-year period
Public Service Commissioner	4 years	8 years in any 16-year period

of public instruction, auditor, and five public service commissioners. Each of these officials holds office for a term of four years. Elected executive-branch officials may serve no more than eight years in any sixteen-year period. Together, the executive-branch officials are in charge of seventeen executive offices, including the departments of Agriculture, Commerce, Transportation, and others.

The governor serves as chief executive officer of Montana. The governor's main duty is reviewing and either approving or rejecting all proposed laws. Montana's governor has the power of line-item veto, which means he or she may reject isolated parts of a bill but approve the rest.

The governor also serves as Montana's main diplomat, greeting visiting politicians and participating in ceremonies when necessary. As commander in chief of the state militia, the governor calls out military troops to protect the public in times of emergency.

▼ Montana's capitol in Helena. The statue of the horseback rider in front of the capitol is of Civil War Union general Thomas Meagher, who became governor of the territory and wrote an early draft of Montana's constitution.

The Legislative Branch

Montana's legislative branch is called the Montana Legislature. It includes the house of representatives, with one hundred members, and the senate, with fifty members. Senators are elected to four-year terms, while

representatives are elected to two-year terms. Like elected officials in the executive branch, legislators may serve no more than eight years in any sixteen-year period.

The state legislature meets in Helena, Montana's state capital, in odd-numbered years. By constitution, each session convenes on January 1 and continues no longer than ninety days, but the legislature or the governor may call special sessions if they are needed.

The legislature's main job is to create new laws. Laws start out as bills that must pass through both the house and the senate. If a bill is approved by both bodies, it is given to the governor for approval or veto.

The Judicial Branch

The main job of the judicial branch is to interpret laws. This important work is done by courts and judges. In Montana, courts are arranged in a three-level system. The actions of courts at lower levels are subject to review by higher-level courts.

The highest level of the judicial branch is the Montana Supreme Court, which has seven members — a chief justice and six associate justices. Supreme Court justices are elected to eight-year terms, and there are no term limits. The Supreme Court's main duty is to review the rulings of the state's lower courts.

Immediately below the Supreme Court are the district courts. There are twenty-two judicial districts and forty district court judges, who are elected to six-year terms. The district courts hear all important cases.

The lowest level of the judicial system includes justices of the peace, city courts, and other special courts that handle smaller cases.

Local Government

At the local level, Montana is split into fifty-six counties. Each county is responsible for its own elections, collection of taxes, road maintenance, law enforcement, and other

Legislature			
House	Number of Members	Length of Term	Term Limits
Senate	50 senators	4 years	8 years in any 16-year period
House of Representatives	100 representatives	2 years	8 years in any 16-year period

local matters. Most counties are governed by an elected board of three county commissioners. Commissioners are elected to six-year terms.

There are also 129 recognized cities and towns (municipalities) in Montana. Municipalities are governed either by a mayor and a city council or by a city council and a city manager.

Tribal Government

In addition to its state and local governments, Montana includes seven federally recognized Native American tribes: the Crow Tribe, the Northern Cheyenne Tribe, the Blackfoot Tribe, the Chippewa Cree Tribe, the Confederated Salish and Kootenai Tribes, the Assiniboin/Sioux Tribe, and the Gros Ventre/Assiniboin Tribe. These tribes are not bound by state laws. They are under the direct supervision of the U.S. Congress. Each tribe has the same power as a state to organize its internal affairs, subject to review by the federal government.

Most tribal governments are organized in much the same way as state and local governments. Officials are elected from within each tribe to represent its interests. Tribes communicate and negotiate with Montana's state government through the Coordinator of Indian Affairs, a person appointed by the governor from a list of five applicants submitted by all tribal councils in the state.

National Representation

Like all states, Montana has two members in the U.S. Senate. It has just one member in the U.S. House of Representatives. Montana's senators are elected to six-year terms; its representative is elected to a two-year term. There are no term limits in the U.S. Congress.

▶ Blackfoot Tribal Chairman Earl Old Person voices his opposition in Billings to a proposed bill which would give ruling power over reservation lands owned by non-tribal members to the state.

Mike Mansfield (1903–2001)

Mike Mansfield, Montana's most distinguished politician, was born in New York but moved to Montana as a child. Between the ages of fourteen and nineteen, he served in the U.S. Navy, Army, and Marine Corps. He then worked in the Butte copper mines for several years before returning to school in 1930. He eventually earned an advanced degree in history and became a full professor at the University of Montana. In 1942, Mansfield was elected as a Democrat to the U.S. House of Representatives, and in 1952, he was elected to the U.S. Senate. He became Senate majority leader in 1961 and held that post until 1977, longer than any other senator in U.S. history. Upon Mansfield's retirement from Congress in 1977, President Jimmy Carter appointed him U.S. ambassador to Japan. Mansfield held that post for twelve years before retiring from politics.

Arts, History, and Outdoors

> There is a blood of vitality that still flows from the land to its literature (and perhaps from the literature back to the land — perhaps the dirt desires stories, as it desires life).
>
> — *Journalist Rick Bass, "On Wilderness and Wallace Stegner," 1997*

Although it is located along the northern border of the continental United States, Montana has a western heart. Montana's culture celebrates the state's frontiersmen, cowboys, and Native American tribespeople. The outdoors is also important to environmentally conscious Montanans, who revel in the wide-open Big Sky lifestyle.

Along with its historical roots, Montana has also developed a broad slate of cultural offerings. Literature, sports, performing arts, and museums provide something for every taste.

Montana's Cultural Center

Missoula is Montana's second-largest city and the state's cultural center. It is home to the University of Montana and has a wealth of offerings that serve the community's diverse and educated population.

Thanks to the university's nationally ranked creative writing program, Missoula is the center of Montana's literary scene. A variety of well-known writers, including novelists James Welch, James Crumley, Ian Frazier, and David James Duncan, make their homes in and around Missoula. Reading and writing seminars are popular

▼ Many Montanans root for the University of Montana Grizzlies football team.

events among Missoula residents, and a variety of bookstores cater to the city's literary community.

The university's sports teams provide another dimension to the Missoula social scene. Known collectively as the Grizzlies, the teams participate in football, basketball, soccer, and other sports throughout the year. Montana has no professional major league sports teams, so college-level sports events tend to draw large and enthusiastic local crowds.

The performing arts are also well represented in Missoula. People come from all over the state to enjoy the Montana Repertory Theatre, the String Orchestra of the Rockies, the Garden City Ballet Company, and many other community performing arts groups.

▲ The C.M. Russell Museum features the art of Charlie Russell and his contemporaries. It contains a vast collection Russell's art and personal objects.

Art Museums

Montana is the home of many well-regarded museums displaying both Western and contemporary art. Perhaps the best-known museum is Great Falls's C. M. Russell Museum, which contains the world's largest collection of works by famed cowboy artist Charles Marion Russell. This museum complex houses Russell's original paintings and sculptures next door to the artist's historic log-cabin studio, which is open to the viewing public.

More Western art is on display at the Museum of the Rockies in Bozeman. This museum contains works by Charles Russell and other artists, as well as traditional Plains Indians crafts, clothing, weapons, and more. Additional Plains Indians artifacts can be seen at the Museum of the Plains Indian on the Flathead Reservation in Browning.

The Montana Historical Society in Helena is another important Montana museum. The Historical Society displays both traditional Western art and contemporary fine art and crafts. Other fine art museums of note include the Yellowstone Art Museum in Billings, the Holter Museum of Art in Helena, and the Art Museum of Missoula.

Historical Sites

Many of Montana's most popular attractions celebrate the state's rich history. Montana's first residents are commemorated at the Pictograph Cave State Historic Site outside Billings, where two-thousand-year-old cave drawings depict buffalo hunts and other aspects of long-ago life on the Plains. Buffalo hunting is also the focus of Ulm

▲ Entrance to Pictograph Cave State Park in the cliffs near Billings. More than four thousand years ago, the area was home to western Indian hunters. Cave paintings and artifacts discovered in the cave document their culture.

DID YOU KNOW?

Dave McNally, Baltimore Orioles pitcher from 1962 to 1974, was born in Billings. McNally is the only pitcher ever to hit a grand slam in a World Series game. The famous hit occurred in Game 3 of the 1970 series against the Cincinnati Reds.

Pishkun in Great Falls and the Buffalo Jump State Historic Site in Madison. These attractions preserve buffalo jumps — high places from which the Montana region's earliest Native peoples drove herds of buffalo to their death in order to harvest their meat, hides, and bones.

Those who are interested in Lewis and Clark's journey may wish to visit Pompey's Pillar National Monument, 25 miles (40 km) east of Billings. William Clark climbed this rock outcropping on his return trip to St. Louis and carved his name and initials into the soft sandstone.

Many attractions highlight Montana's early trading and Indian days. The Fort Union National Historic Site and the city of Fort Benton preserve the atmosphere and artifacts of Montana's fur-trade era. The state's religious roots can be explored at the St. Ignatius Mission on the Flathead Indian Reservation and St. Mary's Mission in Stevensville. Montana's most famous Indian battles are commemorated at the Little Bighorn Battlefield National Monument in the Crow Reservation and the Chief Joseph Battleground, located 15 miles (24 km) south of Chinook.

Montana's mining history is also well represented in the state's offerings. Visitors can explore Bannack, Virginia City, Nevada City, and other ghost towns (settlements that

Grizzlies vs. Bobcats

Rivalry is fierce between the fans of the University of Montana Grizzlies and the Montana State Bobcats. The annual football game between the two schools is sometimes called "The Brawl of the Wild." Emotions run high at this hundred-year-old game, a highlight of the Montana sports scene.

▼ Corps of Discovery leader William Clark's initials are carved into the sandstone of Pompey's Pillar National Monument near Billings.

were once booming cities but were abandoned when the gold rush petered out). Marcus Daly's mansion in Hamilton and William Clark's mansion in Butte are other interesting remnants of Montana's mining era, when the Copper Kings battled for economic and political control of the state.

The Western Experience

Much of Montana's Western character survives into the present. Miles City in southeastern Montana is the present-day heart of cow country. Saddleries and old-time saloons line the town's main street, and rodeos throughout the year allow residents to celebrate their cowboy roots.

Indeed, rodeos are a popular pastime throughout Montana. Most cities and towns of any size host at least one rodeo each year, usually during the summer. Favorites include the Home of Champions Rodeo in Red Lodge, the Bucking Horse Sale in Miles City, the Roundup Rodeo in Livingston, and the Wild Horse Stampede in Wolf Point. At these events, cowboys and cowgirls compete in bull and bronc riding, steer wrestling, calf roping, and barrel racing.

Cowboy and cowgirl wannabes can temporarily live the Western lifestyle at one of Montana's many dude ranches. For a fee, these ranches offer "tenderfeet" the opportunity to help with ranch chores, including real cattle drives and roundups.

Native American powwows are another important part of Montana's cultural landscape. These events range from mostly tribal celebrations to international gatherings. They typically include traditional ceremonies, dances, games, storytelling, and more. Among the largest powwows are North American Indian Days in Browning and Crow Fair on the Crow Reservation.

The Great Outdoors

With its vast expanses of open country, Montana is renowned for its outdoor offerings. Some of the best scenery can be found in Yellowstone National Park in south-central Montana and Glacier National Park in the northwest.

▲ Calf roping is a popular event at the many rodeos held in Montana.

DID YOU KNOW?

Montana's first public bronc riding contest took place in the town of Wolf Point in 1898. The event was won by a cowboy named "Packsaddle Ben" Greenough.

Along Going-to-the-Sun Road, which runs 55 miles (88.5 km) through Glacier, visitors can see bears, glaciers, and gorgeous sunsets. Other significant parks include the northwest's Bob Marshall Wilderness, usually called "the Bob" for short; the Absaroka-Beartooth Wilderness in the state's south-central region; Makoshika State Park in the southeast; and the Charles M. Russell National Wildlife Refuge in east-central Montana.

A booming fish and wildlife population throughout Montana's wilderness areas supports an active fishing and hunting community. Anglers cast for trout and bass in such rivers as the Big Hole and Beaverhead during the summer months. Hunters pursue deer, elk, antelope, and other game animals that are abundant in Montana's forests.

Montanans and visitors engage in many other outdoor activities besides fishing and hunting. Snowmobiling and downhill and cross-country skiing are popular during the winter. Canoeing, kayaking, whitewater rafting, hiking, and camping fill the warmer months.

Fly-Fishing Paradise

Although all types of fishing are popular in Montana, the state is known as a premier fly-fishing destination. In fly fishing, a person casts an unweighted lure and hook that are attached to a fixed-length line and flexible rod. No bait or weights are used.

Montana's fly-fishing culture was romanticized in author Norman Maclean's 1976 novella *A River Runs Through It* and the 1992 movie of the same name. "In our family, there was no clear line between religion and fly fishing," begins the novella, which tells the story of a Montana fly-fishing preacher and his two sons. The photo above shows Vice President Richard Cheney spending some free time in Montana pursuing his favorite sport, fly fishing.

▼ Fly fishing has evolved into an art form in Montana. Premier fly fisherman Bud Lilly shows perfect form on a channel of the Madison River near Three Forks.

Faces of Montana

"It is the resilience and diversity of its meager population that give Montana its fresh face and big heart."

— *Author and Montana resident*
Norma Tirrell, Montana, 2002

Following are only a few of the thousands of people who were born, died, or spent much of their lives in Montana and made extraordinary contributions to the state and the nation.

PIERRE JEAN DE SMET
MISSIONARY

BORN: *January 30, 1801, Belgium*
DIED: *May 23, 1873, St. Louis, MO*

Pierre Jean de Smet was ordained a Jesuit priest in 1827. In 1838, he was sent westward to act as a missionary among Native Americans. He worked in many regions across the Northwest, including Montana, where he ministered to the Salish, Kootenai, Pend d'Oreille, and Blackfoot tribes. De Smet founded St. Mary's Mission, Montana's first Catholic church, and helped establish the St. Ignatius Mission.

MARY FIELDS
STAGECOACH DRIVER

BORN: *1832, Hickman County, TN*
DIED: *1914, Cascade*

Mary Fields was born a slave in rural Tennessee. She was raised by nuns in an orphanage and never married. When the Civil War ended in 1865, Fields became free. She traveled to Cascade, Montana, to join a childhood friend who had entered a convent. A rough woman, Fields upset the calm life of the convent. She soon left to become a stagecoach mail carrier for the fledgling U.S. Postal Service — the first black woman ever to hold this job. Fields's rural Montana route often brought her into contact with bandits, but she was a good shot and always managed to protect herself and the mail. She became famous locally and was known as "Stagecoach Mary" or "Black Mary" until her death in 1914.

CRAZY HORSE
SIOUX WAR CHIEF

BORN: *1842, Rapid Creek, SD*
DIED: *September 5, 1877, Camp Robinson, NE*

From 1865 through 1877, Crazy Horse was a feared warrior in Montana and other frontier regions. He is best remembered for his role in the Battle of the Little Bighorn. On June 25, 1876, Crazy Horse was in command of the warriors who fought and killed Lieutenant Colonel George Custer and his soldiers. Crazy Horse continued to fight U.S. soldiers until 1877, when he was forced to surrender at Red Cloud Agency near Camp Robinson, Nebraska. He died in a struggle with his captors on September 5 of that year.

PLENTY COUPS
CROW CHIEF

BORN: *1848, Billings*
DIED: *March 4, 1932, unknown*

Born in 1848 near present-day Billings, Plenty Coups became a Crow chief by the age of twenty-five or twenty-six. An outstanding warrior, Plenty Coups was also a mediator between the Crow and the U.S. government. He was a tough but fair negotiator who always worked for Crow interests yet was willing to compromise when necessary. For example, after the tribe was forced to move to a reservation, Plenty Coups was one of the first Native people to settle down, start a farm, and build a log cabin. Considered by the U.S. government to be the greatest Native American chief, Plenty Coups was chosen in 1921 to represent all tribes at the burial of the Unknown Soldier in Arlington, Virginia. Today Plenty Coups's house near Pryor, Montana, is the centerpiece of Chief Plenty Coups State Monument, an important state park.

MARTHA JANE "CALAMITY JANE" BURKE
FRONTIERSWOMAN

BORN: *May 1, 1852, Princeton, MO*
DIED: *August 1, 1903, Terry, SD*

Orphaned at an early age, this rebellious frontierswoman wore men's clothing, chewed tobacco, swore, and was a dead shot. She moved to Virginia City, Montana, in 1865 and lived in various towns throughout the state. By the age of 20, she was serving as a scout under Buffalo Bill Cody, another well-known frontier figure. Although Calamity Jane's unladylike ways earned her quite a reputation, she was considered a saint by citizens of Deadwood, South Dakota, where she nursed the sick during a smallpox outbreak.

CHARLES M. RUSSELL
COWBOY ARTIST

BORN: *March 19, 1864, St. Louis, MO*
DIED: *October 24, 1926, Great Falls*

After struggling in obscurity for many years, artist Charles Marion Russell became well known in the early 1900s for his paintings depicting life in wild Montana. Cowboys,

Indians, landscapes, cattle drives, and other typical Montana scenes were his primary subjects. Western sculpture formed a lesser but still well-regarded part of Russell's work. Today Russell's works command up to $1 million apiece. Much of this work can be seen at the

C. M. Russell Museum in Great Falls, which displays the largest single collection of Russell's work anywhere.

JEANNETTE RANKIN
SUFFRAGIST, POLITICIAN

BORN: *June 11, 1880, Missoula*
DIED: *May 18, 1973, Carmel, CA*

Jeannette Rankin first came to prominence through her vocal support of the women's suffrage (right to vote) movement. Her efforts were rewarded in 1914 when Montana gave women the right to vote, six years before the U.S. government did. Rankin then decided to run for a seat in the U.S. House of Representatives. In 1916, she became the first woman ever elected to Congress, where she voted against U.S. entry into World War I. Rankin left Congress in 1919 but was reelected in 1940. In December 1941, Rankin once again voted for peace as the only member of Congress to oppose U.S. entry into World War II.

WILL JAMES
ARTIST AND AUTHOR

BORN: *June 6, 1892, Quebec, Canada*
DIED: *September 3, 1942, Hollywood, CA*

Award-winning author Will James turned out a series of popular Western books and stories from 1924 until his death in 1942. He illustrated many of his own books. Although James did not arrive in Montana until 1927, he passed himself off as a Montana native with a colorful past in his 1930 autobiography, *Lone Cowboy*. The fiction was not discovered until 1967, by which time James was firmly embedded in Montana's lore.

A. B. GUTHRIE, JR.
AUTHOR

BORN: *January 13, 1901, Bedford, IN*
DIED: *April 26, 1991, Choteau*

A. B. Guthrie, Jr., moved with his family to Montana when he was just six months old. He grew up under the "big sky" and developed a love of the land that would eventually shape his life's work. Drawing on his Montana heritage, Guthrie came to be considered one of the foremost writers on the American West. His best-known novels were *The Big Sky*, *The Way West* (for which he won the Pulitzer Prize in 1950), and *These Thousand Hills*.

GARY COOPER
ACTOR

BORN: *May 7, 1901, Helena*
DIED: *May 13, 1961, Los Angeles, CA*

From the mid-1920s until the end of his life, Gary Cooper was an American movie idol. "Coop" appeared in more than 130 movies. He won best-actor Oscars for his work in *Sergeant York* (1941) and *High Noon* (1952). Other notable films included *Morocco* (1930), *A Farewell to Arms* (1932), *Mr. Deeds Goes to Town* (1936), and *Beau Geste* (1939). Cooper was awarded an honorary Oscar in 1960 for "his many memorable screen performances and the international recognition he, as an individual, has gained for the motion picture industry."

NORMAN MACLEAN
AUTHOR

BORN: *December 23, 1902, Clarinda, IA*
DIED: *August 2, 1990, Chicago, IL*

Maclean grew up in Montana as the son of an avid fly fisherman. At the age of seventy-four, Maclean published the acclaimed novella *A River Runs Through It*, which drew upon his boyhood fishing and nature experiences. The novella was made into a 1992 Robert Redford motion picture starring Brad Pitt. Maclean's other works, including *Young Men and Fire* and *USFS 1919: The Ranger, The Cook, and a Hole in the Sky*, also had their roots in Montana culture and lore.

MYRNA LOY
ACTRESS

BORN: *August 2, 1905, Raidersburg*
DIED: *December 14, 1993, New York, NY*

In the mid-1930s, Loy became known for playing an intelligent, sophisticated wife in *The Thin Man* (1934) and five sequels. Loy's immense popularity was demonstrated in 1936 when she was voted Queen of Hollywood. During her career, Loy appeared in 140 films, including *The Best Years of Our Lives* (1946) and *Cheaper by the Dozen* (1950). She was awarded an honorary Oscar in 1991.

JACK HORNER
PALEONTOLOGIST

BORN: *June 15, 1946, Shelby*

Montana native Jack Horner became famous in 1978 when he discovered fossilized dinosaur nesting sites and eggs near Choteau in northwestern Montana. With this discovery, Horner upset long-held theories about dinosaurs' lifestyles. Working since 1982 at Montana State University's Museum of the Rockies, Horner spends the winters teaching and writing and the summers on fossil digs. He also served as the scientific consultant for the *Jurassic Park* movie series and was the inspiration for Dr. Alan Grant, the star of the first movie in the series.

DANA CARVEY
COMEDIAN

BORN: *June 2, 1955, Missoula*

Dana Carvey is best known for his seven-year run (1986–1992) as a cast member on NBC's comedy show *Saturday Night Live*. Carvey's most popular characters were the Church Lady; bodybuilder Hans of the Hans-and-Franz duo; and Garth, cohost of the fictitious TV show *Wayne's World*. Carvey is also known for his dead-on impersonations of politicians, including former U.S. president George Bush.

Montana
History At-A-Glance

1743
François and Louis Joseph de la Vérendrye are the first Europeans to explore present-day Montana.

1805–06
The Lewis and Clark Expedition crosses and recrosses present-day Montana.

1829
The American Fur Company establishes Fort Union.

1846
The Oregon Treaty gives possession of northwest Montana to the United States.

1866
Nelson Story drives 3,000 longhorn cattle from Texas to the plains of present-day Montana.

1877
The Nez Percé tribe clashes with U.S. troops at the Battle of Bears Paw.

1803
The United States purchases the Louisiana Territory from France.

1807
Spaniard Manuel Lisa establishes Fort Manuel Lisa, the first trading post in present-day Montana.

1841
Father Pierre Jean de Smet establishes St. Mary's Mission in the Bitterroot Valley.

1864
Congress creates Montana Territory.

1876
Plains Indian warriors defeat Lieutenant Colonel George Armstrong Custer and his troops at the Battle of the Little Bighorn.

1881
The first major copper mine opens in Butte.

1600	1700	1800

1492
Christopher Columbus comes to New World.

1607
Capt. John Smith and three ships land on Virginia coast and start first English settlement in New World — Jamestown.

1754–63
French and Indian War.

1776
Declaration of Independence adopted July 4.

1787
U.S. Constitution written.

1773
Boston Tea Party.

1777
Articles of Confederation adopted by Continental Congress.

1812–14
War of 1812.

United States
History At-A-Glance

1883
The Northern Pacific Railroad is completed through Montana.

1900-20
Farmers flock to Montana.

1940
Construction of Fort Peck Dam is completed.

1972
Montana's second state constitution is adopted.

1975
Underground mining ceases in Butte.

1989
Montana's centennial celebration includes a three-thousand-head cattle drive through Billings.

1889
Montana is admitted to the Union as the forty-first state.

1918
A severe drought cripples Montana's farming industry.

1951
The discovery of oil reserves in eastern Montana spurs a petroleum boom.

1973
The Montana Strip Mine Reclamation Act and the Major Facility Siting Act are passed.

1983
Anaconda Company closes its Montana operations.

1990s
Timber income declines; tourism and specialized mining gain ground.

1800	1900	2000

1848
Gold discovered in California draws eighty thousand prospectors in the 1849 Gold Rush.

1869
Transcontinental railroad completed.

1929
Stock market crash ushers in Great Depression.

1950–53
U.S. fights in the Korean War.

2000
George W. Bush wins the closest presidential election in history.

1917–18
U.S. involvement in World War I.

1941–45
U.S. involvement in World War II.

1964–73
U.S. involvement in Vietnam War.

1861–65
Civil War.

2001
A terrorist attack in which four hijacked airliners crash into New York City's World Trade Center, the Pentagon, and farmland in western Pennsylvania leaves thousands dead or injured.

▼ Two men steer a horsedrawn freighter wagon for the Babcock and Miles Hardware Company, based in Billings, on a trip near Cinnabar Ranch in this 1886 photograph.

Festivals and Fun for All

Check web site for exact date and directions.

Crow Fair
Crow Agency

This event is the premier powwow of the Plains Indians. With over a thousand authentic tepees set up to accommodate the participants, Crow Fair is sometimes referred to as the "Tepee Capital of the World."
www.indian nations.visitmt.com

Festival of Nations, Red Lodge

This celebration of Red Lodge's diverse heritage highlights the nationalities of the community's first settlers. Three days of events include Scandinavian dances, Scottish games, a Slavic pig roast, Irish fiddlers, and much more multicultural fun.
www.redlodge.com/festival

Custer's Last Stand Reenactment and Little Bighorn Days, Hardin

Over two hundred people act out the clash between Custer's forces and the local Native tribes. The reenactment is held during Little Bighorn Days, a weekend of activities that includes Western-style street dances, quilt shows, parades, chuck wagon feeds, and a carnival.
www.custerslaststand.org

Home of Champions Rodeo, Red Lodge

Billed as one of the great rodeos in America by *National Geographic* magazine, the Home of Champions draws more than four hundred of the country's top cowboys and cowgirls.
www.redlodge.com/rodeo

Jaycee Bucking Horse Sale, Miles City

The main feature of this event is a display and auction of rodeo stock for the Northwest's upcoming rodeo season. The event also features a rodeo, wild horse races, and a street dance.
www.buckinghorsesale.com

Lewis and Clark Festival, Great Falls

From the black powder salute opening to the float trip on the Missouri, this event lets festivalgoers experience life in the time of Lewis and Clark. An educational seminar, a nature walk, and a special historical exhibit round out the weekend activities.
www.corpsofdiscovery.org/festhome.htm

Logger Days, Libby

The highlight of this four-day event is the Montana Lumberjack Championships. Competitions include chainsawing, logrolling, ax throwing, and other traditional lumberjack activities.

www.libbymt.com/events/loggerdays.htm

Montana State Fair, Great Falls

This nine-day fair features everything one expects from a traditional state fair, including a carnival midway, horse racing, a rodeo, livestock exhibits, arts and crafts, and special events.

www.ci.great-falls.mt.us/events/state_fair

Montana State Old-Time Fiddlers Contest, Polson

Top Montana fiddlers compete to determine the best of the best.

www.webmt.net/fiddlers

Mountain Man Rendezvous, Red Lodge

The annual Mountain Man Rendezvous is a historical reenactment of the gatherings of the mountain men during the fur-trade era of the American West.

members.tripod.com/~hrt/ranren01.htm

▶ A teenage cowboy looks for a place to land as he is bucked off his saddle bronco during the Butte High School Rodeo. Unfortunately, his ride fell short of the required eight seconds, so he did not score any points.

North American Indian Days, Browning

North American Indian Days is the largest intertribal powwow in the area. It attracts Native American dancers and drum teams from as far away as Arizona, Oklahoma, Minnesota, and Canada.

www.blackfeetnation.com

Summerfair, Billings

Montana's finest outdoor juried arts and crafts festival features more than one hundred artists and craftspeople from across the country.

http://yellowstone.artmuseum.org

Wild Horse Stampede, Wolf Point

This rodeo is held on the Fort Peck Indian Reservation. Dating back to 1897, it is considered the granddaddy of all Montana rodeos.

www.wolfpoint.com/stamp.htm

Winter Carnival, Red Lodge

Highlights of the Red Lodge Winter Carnival include a snow sculpture competition, torchlight parade, and fire hose race. There are also cardboard vehicle sliding races. Prizes for these vehicles are given for speed and creativity.

www.redlodge.com/Carnival/index.html

Books

Bruchac, Joseph. *Sacajawea: The Story of Bird Woman and the Lewis and Clark Expedition.* San Diego, CA: Silver Whistle, 2000. This historical novel includes traditional Shoshone tales and excerpts from Lewis and Clark's journals.

Gilliland, Hap. *Alone in the Wilderness.* Happy Camp, CA: Naturegraph Publishers, 2001. Tells the story of a present-day Native American high school student who is challenged to spend three months alone in Montana's Beartooth Wilderness.

Horner, John R. *Digging Dinosaurs: The Search That Unraveled the Mystery of Baby Dinosaurs.* New York: Workman Publishing, 1988. Provides an inside look at the work and discoveries of famed paleontologist Jack Horner.

Krehbiel, Randy. *Little Bighorn.* New York: Twenty-First Century Books, 1997. Describes the historical background and events leading up to the conflict, followed by an account of the battle itself, the major participants, and the outcome.

Shirley, Gayle Corbett. *More Than Petticoats: Remarkable Montana Women.* Helena, MT: Falcon Press, 1995. Includes the stories of fourteen women, both famous and little-known, who helped make Montana what it is today.

Stoecklein, David R. *The Montana Cowboy: Legends of the Big Sky Country.* Helena, MT: Stoecklein Publishing, 1998. Tells the story of Montana's legendary cowboys. Packed with full-color photos showing the cowboy way of life.

Web Sites

▶ Official state web site
www.state.mt.us

▶ The Montana Historical Society
www.his.state.mt.us

▶ Montana travel information
www.visitmt.com

Films and Documentaries

McLain, Steven, and Rod Decker. *Montana on My Mind.* Falcon Press Video presents a Vision Media Production, 1995. This film, showing magnificent Montana scenery, seasons, people, places, and events, celebrates the unique beauty and spirit of "the last best state."

Note: Page numbers in *italics* refer to maps, illustrations, or photographs.

A

agate, 6
age distribution, 16
agriculture, 14, 24, *25*, 26–27
airports, 27
Alder Gulch, 10–11
amendments, 28
American bison, *21*
American Indians. *See* Native Americans
Anaconda Copper Company, 13, 15, 43
animals, 6, 7, *20*, 23
art museums, 7, 33–34, 40
attractions. *See also* culture and lifestyle
  festivals, *44*, 44–45, *45*
  Madison Canyon Earthquake Area, 33, *33*
  places to visit, 7

B

Bannack, MT
  development of, 10
  first territorial capital, 30
  Henry Plummer and, 15
  territorial assembly in, 11
  tourist attraction, *26*
Bass, Rick, 32
Battle of the Little Bighorn, 7, 11–13, 39
"Big Sky Country," 4, *4*, 21
bighorn sheep, *20*
Billings, MT, 7, 16, 34, 45
bird (state), 6, *6*
birds, 23
bitterroot, 6
Black Hills, 11–12
blackspotted cutthroat trout, 6, *6*
bluebunch wheatgrass, 6
Bonaparte, Napoleon, 9
books, 46
Browning, MT, 45
buffalo hunting, 34–35
Buffalo Jump State Historic Site, 35
Burke, Martha Jane "Calamity Jane," 39, *39*
Butte High School Rodeo, 45, *45*
Butte, MT, 32, *32*

C

calf roping, *36*
capital. *See* Helena, MT
Carter, Jimmy, 31
Carvey, Dana, 41, *41*
casinos, 18

cattle, 7, *7*, 14, 26
celebrity homes, 17
Charbonneau, Toussaint, 11
Chief Plenty Coups State Monument, 39
cities, 6, 16
Clark Fork River, 23
Clark, William (banker), 13, 30, 36
Clark, William (explorer), *9*, 9–10, 35, *35*
climate, 7, 21
C. M. Russell Museum, 7, 33, 40
Cody, Buffalo Bill, 39
Cohan, Charles C., 6
Congress, 11, 40
Constitution, Montana State, 28, 43
Continental Divide, 22
Cooper, Gary, *40*, 40–41
Coordinator of Indian Affairs, 31
copper, 15
Copper Kings, 13, 30
Corps of Discovery, 9–10, *10*
counties, 30–31
Crazy Horse, 39
Crow Agency, 7, 44
Crow Fair, *18*, 44, *44*
Crow Indians, 39
culture and lifestyle
  art museums, 33–34
  cultural center, 32–33
  historical sites, *34*, 34–35, *35*, 36
  outdoors, 36–37, *37*
  western experience, 36, *36*
Custer, George Armstrong, 12, 39, 42
Custer's Last Stand Reenactment, 44

D

Daly, Marcus, 13, 30, 36
de Smet, Pierre Jean, 12, 38, *38*
dinosaur fossils, 6, 7, 41
documentaries, 46
dude ranches, 36

E

earthquake, 33
economy and commerce
  agriculture, 26–27
  boom and bust, 13–14
  manufacturing, 26
  map, chart of, *25*
  natural resources, 27, *27*
  services, 4, 24, *26*
  trappers, traders, 10
education, 18, 19
employers, top, 24

environmental legislation, 27, 43
European exploration, 8–9
events, *44*, 44–45, *45*
executive branch, 28–29
extremist groups, 19

F

farming. *See* agriculture
fast facts, *6*, 6–7, *7*
Festival of Nations, 44
festivals, *44*, 44–45, *45*
Fields, Mary, 38, *38*
films, 46
fish (state), 6, *6*
fishing, 37, *37*
Flathead Lake, 21, 23
flower (state), 6
fly-fishing, 37, *37*
foreign-born groups, 16
forestry, 26, 27
Fort Benton, 10
Fort Laramie Treaty 1868, 12
Fort Manuel Lisa, 10
Fort Peck Dam, 21, 43
Fort Peck Indian Reservation, 45
Fort Peck Lake, 21, 23
Fort Union National Historic Site, 10, 35
fossils, dinosaur, 6, 7, 41
France, 8–9
frontier lifestyle, 4
fur trade, 10, 24

G

gemstones (state), 6
geography
  description of, 4
  division of jobs from, 17
  of east and west areas, *20*, 20–22, *21*
  land area, 6
  map, *22*
  rivers, lakes, 22–23
  wildlife of, 23
George, W. B., 24
ghost towns, 35–36
Glacier National Park, 6, 7, 37
Going-to-the-Sun Road, 37
gold rush, Montana, 10–11
government, 24, *25*, 26. *See also* politics and government
governor, 29
Granite Peak, 20
grass (state), 6
Grasshopper Creek, 10
Great Centennial Cattle Drive of 1989, 7, *7*
Great Depression, 14
Great Falls, MT, 44, 45
Great Plains region, *21*, 21–22

Greenough, "Packsdale Ben," 36
grizzly bear, 6, 7, *20*
gross state product, 25
Guthrie, A. B., Jr., 40

H

Hardin, MT, 44
Heinze, F. Augustus, 13
Helena, MT, 6, *29*, 30, 34
heritage, *17*, 17
historical sites, *34*, 34–35, *35*, 36
history, 42–43. *See also* Montana
Home of Champions Rodeo, 44
Horner, Jack, 7, 41, *41*
house of representatives, 29–30
Howard, Joseph E., 6
Howard, Joseph Kinsey, 16
Hutterites, 19, *19*

I

Idaho Territory, 11
immigration, 16, 17
Indians. *See* Native Americans
industry, 13–15. *See also* economy and commerce

J

James, Will, 40
Jaycee Bucking Horse Sale, 44
Jefferson, Thomas, 8, 9
Joseph, Nez Percé Chief, 13, *13*
judicial branch, 30

L

la Vérendrye, François de, 8, 42
la Vérendrye, Louis Joseph de, 8, 42
lakes, *22*, 23
land. *See* geography
late hunters, 8
legislation, environmental, 27, 43
legislative branch, 29–30
Lewis and Clark Festival, 44
Lewis and Clark's expedition
  described, 9–10, *10*
  Montana time line, 42
  Monument and, 35, *35*
  portraits of, *9*
  western meadowlark and, 6
Lewis, Meriwether, *9*, 9–10
Libby, MT, 45
lifestyle. *See* culture and lifestyle
line-item veto, 29

Lisa, Manuel, 10
Little Bighorn Days, 44
Little Bighorn National
    Monument, 7, 35
livestock, 26. *See also* cattle
local government, 30–31
Logger Days, 45, *45*
Lone Cowboy (James), 40
Louisiana Purchase, 8, 9, 42
Louisiana Territory, 8, 9
Loy, Myrna, 41, *41*
lumber, 26, 27

M

Maclean, Norman, 37, 41
Madison Canyon Earthquake
    Area, 33, *33*
maiasaur fossils, 6, 7, 41
Major Facility Siting Act,
    27, 43
mammals, 7
mammoth, 8
Mansfield, Mike, 31, *31*
manufacturing, *25*, 26
maps, *5*, *22*, *25*
McNally, Dave, 34
Meagher, Thomas, *29*
Miles City, MT, 36, 44
Militia of Montana, 19
mining
    Copper Kings war, 13
    economy and, 24, *25*, 27, *27*
    gold rush, 10–11
    historical sites of, 35–36
    modern methods of, *15*
    in postwar era, 14–15
missionaries, 12, *12*
Missoula, MT, 32–33
Missouri River, 9, *10*, 22–23
Montana
    fast facts about, *6*, 6–7, *7*
    history of, 8–15, *9*, *10*, *11*, *12*,
        13, *15*
    history time line, 42–43
    maps of, *5*, *22*, *25*
    meaning of name, 20
    resources on, 46
Montana Environmental
    Policy Act, 27
Montana Freemen, 19
*Montana: High, Wide, and
    Handsome* (Howard), 16
Montana Historical Society, 34
Montana Legislature, 29–30
Montana Ordinancy No.1, 28
Montana State Bobcats, 35
Montana State Constitution,
    28, 43
Montana State Fair, 45
Montana State Old-Time
    Fiddlers Contest, 45
"Montana" (state song), 6
Montana Strip Mine
    Reclamation Act, 43

Montana Territory, 11, 42
motto (state), 6
Mountain Man
    Rendezvous, 45
municipalities, 31
Museum of the Rockies, 34, 41
museums, 7, 33–34, 40

N

national monuments, 7, 35, *35*
national parks, 6, 7, 35, 37
national representation, 31
Native Americans
    art of, 34
    Battle of the Little Bighorn,
        11–13
    events, *18*, 44, *44*, 45
    of Montana, 8
    Montana constitution
        and, 28
    Nez Percé, 13, *13*
    notable people, 39
    Pierre Jean de Smet
        and, 38
    population of, 17–18
    powwows, 36
    Sacagawea, 11, *11*
    tribal government, 31, *31*
natural resources, 4, 26, 27.
    See also mining
nests, dinosaur, 7, 41
Nez Percé, 13, *13*, 42
North American Indian
    Days, 45
Northern Pacific Railway,
    13, 43

O

oil, 14–15, *27*, 43
Old Person, Chief, *31*
"On Wilderness and Wallace
    Stegner" (Bass), 32
Oregon Treaty of 1846, 10, 42
outdoors, 36–37, *37*

P

parks. *See* national parks
people, notable, 32, 38–41
Pictograph Cave State
    Historic Site, 34, *34*
Plenty Coups, Chief, 39, *39*
Plummer, Henry, 15
politics and government, 11,
    28–31, *29*, *31*
Polson, MT, 45
Pompey's Pillar National
    Monument, 35, *35*
ponderosa pine, 6, *6*
population
    changes in, 13–14, 15
    of Montana, 6
    statistics, 16–17
powwows, 36, 44
Protestantism, 18, 19

R

racial background, 17, *17*
railroads, 13, 43
rainfall, 21
Rankin, Jeannette, 7, 40, *40*
Red Lodge, 44, 45
Religion
    missionaries, 12, *12*
    Pierre Jean de Smet, 38
    places to visit, 35
    types of, 18–19
reservations, 12–13, 17–18
resources, 46. *See also*
    natural resources
A River Runs Through It
    (Maclean), 37, 41
rivers, *22*, 22–23
Road Agents, 15
Rocky Mountains, *20*,
    20–21, 23
rodeos, 36, 44, 45, *45*
Roman Catholicism, 19
Roundup, MT, 7
Russell, Charles Marion, 7, 33,
    34, *39*, 39–40, *40*

S

Sacagawea, 11, *11*
St. Mary's Mission
    building, *12*
sapphire, 6
Saturday Night Live, 41
school, 19
senate, 29–30
services, 4, 15, 24, *25*, 26
Shoshone, 11
song (state), 6
sports, 32, *32*, 33, 34
"Stagecoach Mary", 38, *38*
statehood, 13
Steinbeck, John, 20
Stillwater Mining Company, 26
Story, Nelson, 14, 42
Strip Mine Reclamation
    Act, 27
strip mining, 27
Summerfair, 45
Supreme Court, 30

T

temperature, 7, 21
timber, 27
time line, 42–43
Tirrell, Norma, 38
tourism, 24, *26*
traders, 10
trappers, 10
*Travels with Charley: In
    Search of America*
    (Steinbeck), 20
tree (state), 6, *6*
tribal government, 31, *31*

U

Union, 6, 43
United States, 9, 10, 42–43
United States Constitution, 42
University of Montana, 32, 33
University of Montana
    Grizzlies, *32*, 33, 35

W

web sites, 46
western meadowlark, 6, *6*
Wild Horse Stampede, 45
wildlife, 23
Winter Carnival, 45
Wolf Point, MT, 45
women's suffrage
    movement, 40

Y

Yellowstone National Park,
    7, 37
Yellowstone River, 23